33517 - THE UNTOLD STORY OF PRIVATE F. L. HUTCHINSON

SANDI K. WILSON

33517 - THE UNTOLD STORY OF PRIVATE F. L. HUTCHINSON

Copyright © 2025 by Sandi K. Wilson
Cover Artwork by SKW Publishing
Cover Design by SKW Publishing
Photographs by Family Archives

ISBN 978-1-7386126-0-4 Paperback
ISBN 978-1-7386126-1-1 E-Book

All rights reserved. No part of this book may be reproduced in any manner whatsoever without written permission except in the case of brief quotations embodied in critical articles and reviews.

First Printing 2024
Second Printing 2025
© SKW Publishing

CONTENTS

Dedication
ix

– From the Author
1

1 – Kaye's Story
3

2 – Departure to War
9

3 – Maadi Camp
14

4 – El Aine, Syria
19

5 – First Taste of Action
24

6 – Battle of El Alamein
29

7 – Prisoner of War
33

8 – The Nino Bixio
37

9 – Campo 57
41

10 – The Church
52

11 – Into the Dark
55

12 – Polish Camp and Mines
60

13 – Stalag 8B/344
66

14 – A Soldier's Story
72

15 – The Long March
76

16 – Liberation
82

17 – Repatriation
85

18 – Returning Home to NZ
96

19 – Life and Legacy
101

– Private F.L. Hutchinson
104

– References
105

– About the Author
107

DEDICATION

To Kaye & Rayna

The 'perfect ones!'
Thank you for trusting me with this monumental task.

Sandi xx

FROM THE AUTHOR

Some stories live quietly in the background of family memory—until one day, they step forward and ask to be told.

This is one of those stories.

I'm Sandi Wilson, granddaughter of Private Frank Leonard Hutchinson: Len to most, Hutch to many, Grandpa to me. Like countless others, he was issued a number during the war: 33517. To his captors, he may have been a statistic. To us, he was, and remains, irreplaceable.

What began as a small act of remembrance turned into a deeply personal pilgrimage. I followed my grandfather's footprints through deserts and battlefields, across rail lines and prison camps, through diary pages and whispered family tales. Some of these stories were handed down in fragments over the dinner table. Others were stitched together from old records, fellow soldiers' accounts, and long hours of quiet research. Not every detail can be perfectly confirmed—some memories stretch wider than the facts—but I've done my best to honour both truth and heart.

Len's journey spans oceans and nations, but his soul is found in his steadfast courage, in the friendships that held, and in the faith that endured even behind barbed wire.

This book is not just a war story. It's a love story. It's a legacy. And it's my thank-you.

Thank you, Grandpa, for your bravery, your quiet strength, and the life you came home to build. You were more than a soldier.

You were, and always will be, our hero.

Sandi K. Wilson

CHAPTER 1

KAYE'S STORY

In 1995, amidst a significant upheaval in my life, an unexpected adventure unfolded—an adventure that traced its roots back to the early days of World War II when I was just three weeks old. At that tender age, my father, Frank Leonard Hutchinson, known as Len, departed Northcote, Auckland, as a private in the New Zealand Army. After a few weeks of fighting in 1942, he was captured in the Libyan desert and sent to Campo 57, a Prisoner of War camp situated in the Udine area of Northern Italy.

Within the harsh confines of Campo 57, Len formed a lasting friendship with another Kiwi, Fred Such, from Onehunga, Auckland—a bond that endured for 40-50 years until their deaths. The camp, though cruel, became a haven for the men, where mail and parcels from home brought solace. Treasured photos of family and friends, sent by my mother, Norma, adorned the barracks. These images, often marked with Stalag numbers and unusual inscriptions, became precious relics, testaments to the resilience of the human spirit.

A postcard sent by Len during his time as a POW.
© Family Archives.

During their time together, my mother sent a family photo to Dad, prompting Fred's curiosity about each sister. In the close-knit barracks, the men knew one another's families intimately, sharing stories of loved ones left behind. Fred, pointing to one of my aunts, humorously declared, "I like the look of that one. Save her for me when we get back to New Zealand!" The camaraderie between Dad and Fred deepened through numerous experiences and changes in various camps, solidifying their enduring friendship.

Amidst this backdrop, young English individuals wrote letters to single POWs, initiating a pen pal friendship between Fred and Beryl Brown from South London. Liberation marked a poignant journey as Fred, Dad, and two other Kiwis sought out Beryl and her family in London to express gratitude. This encounter forged a lasting friendship, with family members travelling across the ocean to visit each other. During this time, POWs were billeted with English families, fostering connections that endured even after the war. The Brown family welcomed Fred, while Dad found shelter with an elderly couple in London.

Upon Dad and Fred's return to New Zealand in 1945, a local dance in Northcote introduced Fred to my Aunty Tuppy, the sister from the family photo. The evening before my fourth birthday marked the beginning of a unique romance, and within a year, Fred and Aunty Tuppy were married— a love story that blossomed in the challenging circumstances of Campo 57. Dad and Uncle Fred became brothers-in-law.

Fast forward to 1995, with both my mother and father having passed away. Fred, aware of my trip to the United Kingdom for the 50th anniversary of the war's end, requested that I represent him and Aunty Tup with the Brown family. Honoured and proud, I travelled to the UK with my son and daughter-in-law, basing ourselves in Wales. A planned gathering with the Brown family on 21

May 1995 and a poignant visit to Nana Brown's home brought forth emotional moments. Sitting in the corner chair, Nana Brown noted the exact spot where my dad had sat 50 years ago, a poignant connection across time.

Attending the VE Parade on Chestnut Avenue, we immersed ourselves in the historical re-enactments and displays, capturing the essence of that unforgettable day. Notably, the British Legion members, sipping specially brewed 1945 Bass Beer in a separate enclosure, became a unique memento for Fred.

Returning to New Zealand a few years later, settling on the North Shore, I delved into researching Campo 57, where Dad and Fred spent over a year of their lives. With assistance from my son Tony, who lived in London, we uncovered valuable information through the Internet. A kind lady in Northland, New Zealand, provided directions and shared photos, contributing to our understanding of the camp.

Kaye and Laurie with some of the locals at Premariacco, Italy. © Family Archives.

33517 - THE UNTOLD STORY OF PRIVATE F. L. HUTCHINSON

In 2009, a significant year marked by my overseas adventure, I journeyed to Campo 57 with my eldest son, Laurie. Contacting a local resident, Romina, whose family lived on the camp's former land, she played a crucial role in organising our visit. Despite language barriers, the locals welcomed us with pride, sharing stories of the camp's history. A visit to the memorial church, rebuilt from the POWs' efforts, became a deeply emotional experience. Anzac poppies laid in honour of Dad, Uncle Fred, and others on the church's altar were symbolic of a connection spanning generations.

The story of the church's reconstruction, involving Father Loughan from New Zealand, added a poignant layer to our journey. As a young man and POW in the camp, he aspired to become a priest upon his return to New Zealand. His return to take mass in the rebuilt church, documented in the Campo P.G. 57 book, attested to the enduring impact of the camp. A plaque on the church's front commemorated the English, New Zealand, Australian, and Canadian POWs, a testament to a community that remembered and honoured their sacrifice with a special annual mass.

Reflecting on the time frame of Dad and Fred's internment, from November 1942 to December 1943, I was reminded of Fred's diaries, recounting their march out of camp as the Italians handed them over to the Germans. Recreating that journey and witnessing the hills where resistance fighters and escaped POWs sought refuge, we embraced the profound history surrounding us.

"Well Dad, although you didn't talk much about the war, and the little you did share with us stirred my curiosity, I am so proud that myself and two of your grandsons have been able to see where you spent such a critical thirteen months of your life. It was special for me to share the memory of being there and standing on land in a foreign country where you and Uncle Fred had been in horrendously difficult and harsh times. There is little left of the camp itself, but by placing poppies on the altar in the church, I have left a remembrance of you and Uncle Fred in this faraway and yet important place."

These special memories, forever etched in my heart, were a testament to the enduring bonds forged in the crucible of war.

Kaye Clewett, née Hutchinson, 2009.

CHAPTER 2

DEPARTURE TO WAR

The Hutchinson household in the heart of Auckland's North Shore was a bustling hub of activity, filled with the usual sounds of a newborn's cries and the soothing murmurs exchanged between a new father and mother. Private Frank Leonard Hutchinson, known affectionately as Len, stood in the doorway of the modest home, gazing at the scene before him with a mix of love and duty etched across his face. His wife Norma cradled their three-week-old daughter Kaye in her arms, a beacon of hope and promise in a world overshadowed by the looming spectre of war.

Len, a man with a tall, slim frame, easy and laid back, but with a strength and determination that rivalled any other soldier, was about to embark on a journey that would forever alter the course of his life. Born and raised in the gorgeous landscapes of New Zealand, Len grew up with a sense of adventure coursing through his veins. As a young man, he met and fell in love with Norma, a woman whose strength matched his own, and together, they began to build a life filled with dreams of a future beyond the horizon.

Len and Norma Hutchinson. © Family Archives.

The call to serve came echoing through the valleys of their tranquil existence, disrupting the peace they had so carefully cultivated via conscription. World War II had cast its long shadow over the world, and Len, like many others, understood the duty to answer that call.

After his initial sign-up, Len would be transferred to Papakura Training Camp, where he would train alongside other men who were now considered soldiers. Whilst at the camp, he contracted whooping cough and spent a few weeks in the Army hospital recovering. When he arrived home, it was to the news that he and Norma would be welcoming their first baby.

Kaye was born on August 17, 1941. Thus, Len and Norma's lives had changed forever. With the help of his mother, May, Len knew that Kaye would be a comfort and a great well of hope and love to his beloved Norma.

The day he left Auckland for Wellington, the air was thick with a mixture of emotions—love, fear, and a quiet resolve that resonated within Len's heart.

Babe in arms, Norma walked with Len to Northcote Point, kissed her beloved husband, and waved goodbye to him as he boarded the ferry to take him to the train station in Auckland.

He wouldn't see the tears that ran down Norma's face as she whispered a prayer for her husband's safety and the hope that he would return one day to resume his role as husband, and now, father.

The train journey to Wellington was a sombre one, punctuated by the distant cries of farewells and the rhythmic clatter of metal against metal. Len's thoughts oscillated between the family he left behind and the uncertainty that lay ahead. In Wellington, a bustling harbour city teeming with soldiers in various stages of preparation, after parading through the city, Len boarded His Majesty's New Zealand Troop Ship SS Aquitania, which would carry him far from the shores of his homeland.

The journey to Egypt was a test of endurance, both physically and mentally. Len, along with his fellow soldiers, navigated the vast expanse of the ocean, bound for a destination obscured by the fog of war. The ship cut through the waves, carrying them towards an uncertain fate. The camaraderie forged during those long, tedious days at sea would become the foundation upon which the soldiers built their resilience.

Finally, the ship docked in Egypt on a fateful day in October 1941. Len disembarked at Port Tewfik (now Port Taofik) at the southern entrance to the Suez Canal. From there, his journey continued westward via train to Maadi Camp in Cairo, some 90 miles away. Len stepped onto foreign soil, greeted by the warm winds of the desert and the distant echoes of a war that raged beyond the horizon. Maadi Camp, with its sandy surroundings and makeshift barracks, became Len's new home—a place where the realities of war began to unfold before his eyes.

In the heart of the desert, Private Frank Leonard Hutchinson took his first steps into the tumultuous world of war, unknowingly setting in motion a series of events that would shape his destiny in ways he could never have imagined.

His Majesty's Troop Ship SS Aquitania, Wellington Harbour, NZ © nzhistory.govt.nz

CHAPTER 3

MAADI CAMP

In the fall of 1941, Len's journey led him to Maadi, an expansive canvas of sand slopes that would become the backdrop to a pivotal phase in his military odyssey. The camp, strategically situated near Cairo, offered a breathtaking panorama. To the east, the vast expanse of the desert stretched out, providing ample room for route marches and manoeuvres. To the north, the Mokattam Hills framed the distant silhouette of the Cairo Citadel, and to the west, Maadi village descended toward the Nile, with the Pyramids of Gizeh etching their enigmatic presence on the distant skyline.

33517 - THE UNTOLD STORY OF PRIVATE F. L. HUTCHINSON

Maadi Camp with the bell-shaped tents. © A. Hedley Sr.

Maadi became a home of sorts for the 18th Battalion, a melting pot of diverse experiences that unfolded over more than six months. The routine, though, started with a focus on safety within the camp. Orders were clear: rifles and arms were to be guarded diligently, chained to tent poles at night, locked, with bolts removed and placed under pillows. The expansive borders of the camp proved porous, and local traders seized opportunities arising from both the soldiers' patronage and the burgeoning black market fueled by wartime demand and anti-British sentiments.

Amidst these challenges, 18 Battalion, positioned on the camp's periphery, faced unique vulnerabilities. Egyptian thieves operated under the cover of darkness, stealthily making off with petrol tins, truck parts, and even rifles. In response, the resourceful battalion erected a booby-trapped fence armed with flares—a makeshift sentry that would light up at the first hint of disturbance.

Training commenced immediately upon arrival, with daily route marches and a focus on desert warfare preparedness. As dawn broke, soldiers engaged in a ten-minute run before breakfast, followed by rigorous route marches that progressively increased in distance to level up their fitness. The harsh reality of desert warfare was mirrored in the stringent water conservation measures, with every soldier's water bottle scrutinised by the watchful eyes of the sergeant.

Life in Maadi wasn't confined to military drills. Soldiers were granted leave to Cairo, where the bustling markets of the Mousky bazaar beckoned exploration. The Egyptian currency became second nature, and soldiers navigated the city, hopping onto the rickety Maadi bus service—a character in its own right, seemingly held together by prayer and string.

Cairo offered a range of diversions. Soldiers could relax in British servicemen's clubs, brave the lively bars and cabarets, or venture into the less respectable quarters, like the Wagh el Birket, where every imaginable vice was on display at varying prices.

The Assistant Provost Marshal's cautionary talk about Cairo's 'in bounds' and 'out-of-bounds' areas, marked on a street map resembling a sea of red with a small white island, did little to deter the allure of forbidden zones for some adventurous souls.

Len, a part of A Company, embarked on a peculiar mission that led the battalion to Tura, two miles up the Nile from Maadi. There, hidden in caves in the hillside, lay one of the Middle East's largest ammunition dumps. This obscure assignment became a significant chapter in the battalion's narrative, reinforcing the British guard until permanent reinforcements arrived.

Tura, with its ancient limestone quarry, bore witness to history as a key source of materials for the construction of the Giza Pyramids and the Great Sphinx. The soldiers, amidst the challenges and unexpected turns, discovered layers of history beneath the surface of their wartime experience.

Maadi Hospital Camp. © National Library of New Zealand, DA-06827-F.

Len's personal journey took an unexpected turn in early December of 1941. While transferring from Tura caves to Northern Infantry Training Depot, Maadi, burdened with his complete baggage, he strained himself severely. A 38-day hospital stay followed, marking a chapter of recovery amid the ever-evolving story of 18 Battalion in the heart of Maadi. The camaraderie forged, the challenges overcome, and the blend of history and humanity made Maadi a unique chapter in the tapestry of Len's wartime experience.

CHAPTER 4

EL AINE, SYRIA

On 10 May 1942, Len marched into the 18th Battalion, at the time enjoying a rest in El Aine, Syria.

In the early 1940s, Syria stood at the crossroads of history, shaped by the complexities of French mandate rule and the transformative winds of World War II. The French mandate, established in the aftermath of World War I, cast a shadow over Syria's aspirations for self-determination. Tensions between the local population and French authorities simmered, and the struggle for independence gained momentum. In 1941, the theatre of war arrived on Syrian soil as Allies, including Free French and British forces, clashed with Vichy French forces, ultimately paving the way for the expulsion of colonial powers.

Amidst the political upheaval, Syrian society exhibited a rich tapestry of diversity, with various ethnic and religious communities coexisting within its borders. Traditional societal structures, influenced by historical norms, faced the challenges of evolving under colonial rule. Nomadic and tribal elements persisted, particularly in the expansive Syrian Desert, while urbanisation began to reshape social dynamics. The quest for independence ignited a sense of national identity, fostering unity among Syrians who sought to break free from foreign dominion.

Syria's topography remained a testament to its geographical diversity. From the coastal plains to the mountainous regions and the vast deserts, the land bore witness to the ebb and flow of history. The mountainous terrain, including the Anti-Lebanon and Lebanon ranges, held both cultural and strategic significance.

El Aine, Syria. ©Alexander Turnbull Library, DA-13237.

Meanwhile, the arid expanses of the Syrian Desert, home to nomadic Bedouin communities, retained an ancient allure. As the sun cast its shadow over this diverse landscape, Syria's destiny unfolded against the backdrop of a changing world.

From the time the 18th Battalion arrived at El Aine, it mounted a full guard on its camp, the first since leaving New Zealand. This was not just ornamental but protection against the Syrians, who enjoyed wide notoriety as thieves and had a particular liking for army equipment. At the beginning of May, with the introduction of summer working hours (7 a.m. to 12.30 p.m.), the afternoons became the men's own to do pretty much what they pleased. A little desultory cricket was played, but it was too hot for football. Some men explored the villages, and some went off visiting friends in other units, and more and more took advantage of daily swimming trips to the source of the Orontes River, which springs from under a cliff in a deep gorge, forms a small pool, and from there goes thundering down the gorge to the plain. It is a wild and rugged but magnificent spot. The snow water made you gasp when you plunged into it, and most of the swimmers found a couple of 'just in and outs' quite enough. The recognised thing after a dip was to climb the cliff to some ancient fortified (and pretty inaccessible) caves, then to come down and brave the icy water again before going home.

Back at El Aine, the 18th Battalion, to its irritation, found that it was to do more work on the defences, which it thought it had left behind. Interspersed with this work was a little range firing, which everyone enjoyed, and anti-gas training, which everyone hated. However, the general tone in the unit was perkier than before because now, for the first time, there was talk of a wonderful holiday camp in Beirut, on the Mediterranean, over the other side of the Lebanons; the whole unit, [said the rumour], was going there to spend a week swimming and enjoying the delights of city life. Those whose duties had already taken them to Beirut spoke glowingly of the town—a handsome, well-to-do place with everything you needed for a good time. The prospect was most encouraging. Fifty men from the battalion, who were to be camp guards at El Aine while the rest were at Beirut, went to the holiday camp on 5 June with the Maori Battalion. They were the lucky ones. They had their holiday and returned on 12 June. The same day, the rest of the battalion crowded into ASC lorries and rode away, in the highest of high spirits, over the Lebanon to Beirut.

Back in the familiar embrace of Maadi Camp, the atmosphere was charged with a mixture of anticipation and trepidation. The soldiers, hardened by training and strengthened by the bonds formed in El Aine, faced the challenge of preparing for active engagement in the theatre of war. The camp buzzed with activity as supplies were checked, strategies devised, and the resilience of the battalion tested.

Preparations for their involvement in the war became a collective effort. Len, alongside his fellow soldiers, meticulously readied themselves for the uncertainties that lay ahead. As the battalion geared up for the next phase, the echoes of past battles and the weight of future responsibilities hung heavy in the air.

33517 - THE UNTOLD STORY OF PRIVATE F. L. HUTCHINSON

For Private Frank Leonard Hutchinson, the journey with the 18th Battalion signified more than a mere change in assignment—it was a shift from the relative calm of training to the impending storm of actual combat. The camaraderie formed in El Aine would soon be tested on a grander scale, as Len and his comrades prepared to face the crucible of war in the unforgiving landscapes of North Africa.

CHAPTER 5

FIRST TASTE OF ACTION

The day dawned over the desolate landscape of Minqar Qaim, a place that would etch itself into Len Hutchinson's memory as the stage for his initiation into the brutal realities of war. The sun painted the sky with hues of orange and pink, casting a deceptive tranquillity over the arid terrain. Little did Len and his comrades of the 18th Battalion know that this day would be eternally marked by the thunderous roar of engines and the piercing wails of falling bombs.

The battalion, positioned strategically in the desert, found itself thrust into the heart of the conflict as German aircraft descended from the sky like vultures circling their prey. The suddenness of the attack caught them off guard, turning the serene landscape into a theatre of chaos. Dust clouds billowed into the air as explosions rocked the ground, a symphony of destruction playing out against the backdrop of the unforgiving desert.

Len, along with his fellow soldiers, scrambled for cover, their senses overwhelmed by the cacophony of warfare. The once-distant thunder of artillery now rumbled in their chests, and the acrid smell of burning sand mingled with the metallic tang of fear. The reality of combat unfolded with startling clarity, punctuated by the staccato rhythm of gunfire and the distant screams of men caught in the crossfire.

In the chaos, Len's training kicked in, and instinct guided his movements. The barren landscape offered little refuge, and the soldiers, now realising the vulnerability of their position, sought whatever cover they could find. The German bombing run at Minqar Qa'im marked a baptism of fire for Len and his comrades, a brutal introduction to the unpredictable and perilous nature of war.

The minutes felt like hours as the relentless assault continued. The earth trembled beneath the weight of each explosion, and the once-sturdy resolve of the soldiers began to waver. Yet, amidst the chaos, bonds were forged in the crucible of adversity. Soldiers, bound by a shared struggle, looked to one another for reassurance and support, finding strength in the unity that blossomed amid the onslaught.

Surrounded by fast-moving German forces and facing certain defeat, the New Zealand Division had no choice but to launch a breakout on the night of June 27-28, 1942.

The commander of the 2NZEF, Major-General Bernard 'Tiny' Freyberg, had initially set up defensive positions at Mersa Matruh, a coastal town around 450 km west of Cairo. Seeking a more mobile role for his division, he moved the New Zealanders further south to Minqar Qaim.

Eight months before the breakout, the Division had taken heavy losses during Operation Crusader. "With 879 dead and 1700 wounded, the New Zealand Division had fought its most costly battle of the war", notes NZHistory. "In February 1942, at the New Zealand government's insistence, they moved to Syria to recover."

'First Taste of Action,' painting of Minqar Qa'im.
© *archives.govt.nz.*

However, when the German commander, Field Marshal Rommel, launched a fresh offensive in the Western Desert, the Division was recalled to North Africa to face the advancing forces. Within days, rapidly advancing German forces had cut the New Zealanders off from Allied forces to the east. The Division soon found itself surrounded and cut off from any help.

Ammunition levels were dire – the artillery only had enough shells for one more day. This set of circumstances led the Division to develop a bold plan: to break out of the encirclement. Led by the 4th Brigade, after midnight on 28 June, the New Zealand Division burst through the ring of German forces.

Taking the German forces by surprise, the New Zealanders bayoneted and shot their way through the enemy. In the confusion that followed, the Division caught a German medical unit and its patients in the battle, killing many of them. This incident has led some to allege that New Zealand troops committed a war crime. Others point to evidence that the troops involved were not aware that the German personnel they were attacking were from a medical unit.

The breakout of infantry was followed by hundreds of vehicles, driving at full pace with orders not to stop for anything.

As the dust settled and the echoes of the bombing run faded into the stillness of the desert, Len Hutchinson stood amidst the aftermath, his senses heightened and his perspective forever altered. The harsh realities of war had etched themselves into his consciousness—the fragility of life, the unpredictability of conflict, and the profound camaraderie that emerged in the crucible of adversity. The experience at Minqar Qaim marked not only Len's first taste of action but also a profound realisation that the path ahead was fraught with challenges that demanded resilience, courage, and an unyielding spirit.

The breakout at Minqar Qaim was one of many intense battles fought in North Africa during the Second World War.

The Division then withdrew to the Alamein Line. Len then took part in the First Battle of El Alamein in July 1942.

CHAPTER 6

BATTLE OF EL ALAMEIN

In the scorching summer of 1942, Len Hutchinson and the 18th Battalion found themselves on the precipice of one of the defining moments of World War II—the First Battle of El Alamein. The vast expanse of sand stretched before them, a canvas upon which the fate of nations would be written in the blood and sweat of soldiers.

The 18th Battalion, battle-hardened from their earlier ordeals, stood resolute in the face of the approaching storm. El Alamein, a name that would echo through the annals of history, beckoned them to a theatre of war fraught with uncertainty. Len, alongside his comrades, felt the weight of the impending conflict as they dug trenches and fortified their positions, their eyes scanning the horizon for signs of the enemy.

The battle commenced with the thunderous roar of artillery, an overture to a symphony of destruction that would unfold in the moonlit desert. Len's senses were heightened as the night sky erupted in flashes of gunfire, casting an eerie glow over the shifting dunes. The 18th Battalion, entrenched in their positions, braced themselves for the onslaught.

Amidst the chaos and the deafening roar of battle, camaraderie flourished among the soldiers of the 18th Battalion. Bonds formed in the crucible of conflict, as shared hardships and the spectre of mortality forged connections that transcended the superficial. In the heart of El Alamein, soldiers became brothers, their collective strength greater than the sum of their parts.

The First Battle of El Alamein. © Wikipedia.

As the battle raged on, the 18th Battalion, with Len among its ranks, became a symbol of resilience in the face of overwhelming odds. The desert sands bore witness to

33517 - THE UNTOLD STORY OF PRIVATE F. L. HUTCHINSON

acts of valour and sacrifice as the 18th Battalion, like an unyielding bastion, held their ground against the ebb and flow of the conflict.

Then came the fateful day of July 15, 1942, etched in history, when Len and many comrades became unfortunate captives after the Germans overran their position at Ruweisat Ridge. The lack of tank and heavy artillery support proved costly, and Len was marked as missing in action.

An infantryman's diary recounts the intensity of the battle: "The tanks, having knocked out our guns, came rumbling and clanking towards us with nothing to stop them. Their machine guns were going all the time at anyone they saw moving, while behind them were German infantry and more tanks. We could do nothing but keep hoping that some of our own tanks would turn up to the rescue; alas, we were alone in the desert."

No one had visualised or even entertained being captured, least of all after the successful previous attack. It came as a shock to see the men with their hands up, and as one man puts it, "I think we all felt silly and self-conscious."

Those captured 18 days later at Ruweisat Ridge experienced a carry-over of hard feelings from Minqar Qaim. Some were expressly asked whether they had taken part in the Minqar Qaim action. Whether from this cause or not, although there was no brutality, the experiences of prisoners from the moment of their capture at Ruweisat until their arrival in a back area were unpleasant enough. Men of

18 and 19th Battalions, after a search for arms, were herded back a mile or two to a holding area, where there was a count and officers were taken off for interrogation. The march back then continued until late that night, by which time all had raging thirsts and a number had collapsed. There was no food and almost no water that night, nor was there any until, completely exhausted, they reached transport later the next morning.

Eventually, the transport arrived and took them to the prisoner-of-war cage at Daba. The journey marked the end of the chapter at El Alamein, leaving Len and his comrades to contemplate the cost of war and the uncertainty that lay ahead in captivity. In the crucible of El Alamein, Len and his comrades discovered a strength within themselves that transcended the physical and forged a legacy that would endure long after the echoes of battle faded into the sands of the Egyptian desert.

CHAPTER 7

PRISONER OF WAR

Under the relentless Libyan sun, Private Frank Leonard Hutchinson, known as Len, found himself ensnared in the unpredictable grip of war. The aftermath of a brutal engagement left Len and his comrades strewn across the arid canvas of the Libyan desert, the echoes of conflict still lingering in the air. In the harsh reality of war's capricious fate, Len, battle-weary but resolute, realised he was now a prisoner of war.

Captured by faceless enemies, Len's world transformed from the camaraderie of the 18th Battalion to the stark desolation of captivity. Faces obscured by the desert sun, his captors herded the prisoners together, marking the beginning of a journey that would test their endurance and resilience to the fullest.

The trek across the unforgiving Libyan desert became an ordeal, a gruelling march under the scorching sun that seemed to stretch endlessly in every direction. The prisoners, spirits dampened but unbroken, trudged through the shifting sands. For Len and his fellow captives, this journey became a testament to the indomitable human spirit in the face of adversity.

After hours of marching, Len and his comrades were loaded onto a truck and taken to the transit camp at Daba—a mere piece of desert enclosed by barbed wire, once a British cage, now in the hands of the Germans. The cool evening sea breeze offered a moment of relief to men parched and nearly insensible from the twenty-mile trek across the desert. Officers and men were separated, subjected to another search, and given meagre rations of water and biscuits. Most men lay on the soft sand, trying to find solace in sleep.

It was during this desert internment that Len encountered the tall, foreboding presence of Fred Such. Little did he know then that his friendship with Fred would blossom into an enduring bond and brotherhood.

Len's journey continued by truck via Tobruk to Benghazi in Cyrenaica, Libya. Packed tightly in large Italian trucks, the prisoners endured the coastal road for four to five days, with nightly stops at barbed-wire pens. The Italian guards, at times brutal, rationed scarce food, but the prisoners were thankful for the water, a stark contrast to the torturous thirst they endured in the early days of captivity.

33517 - THE UNTOLD STORY OF PRIVATE F. L. HUTCHINSON

Arriving at Tobruk's large prisoner-of-war compound, the scene was chaotic. Shanties, blanket-huts, and tents sprawled haphazardly, housing a diverse mix of prisoners—South African Blacks, Indians, Gurkhas, Siamese, Springboks, Tommies, and Kiwis. Conventional values evaporated as individuals from different walks of life lived cheek by jowl, forging a unique camaraderie.

As the prisoners settled into their new reality, wood fires illuminated the encampment, creating an exotic atmosphere under the stars. Amid discussions about food, escape plans, and endless rumours, Len and his fellow captives found ways to endure the hardships. However, dysentery spread, queues for the latrines were unending, and the camp's conditions deteriorated.

In early August, group leaders sought better rations from the Italian commandant, assuming a lengthy stay. However, the camp was abruptly cleared, and the prisoners were transported by truck—600 to a waiting ship and the rest to the main Benghazi prisoner-of-war collection centre.

The journey brought most other ranks to a camp southeast of Benghazi, nicknamed the 'Palm Tree camp.' The conditions were harsh—stones served as beds, latrines overflowed, and hygiene was a distant luxury. Despite the challenges, men found solace in shared domestic activities, enhancing the palatability of their meagre rations and distracting them from the surrounding misery.

Camp 116 – Palm Tree Camp. © H.R. Dixon.

As the days passed, the situation grew grimmer. Nights cooled, sandstorms and rain exposed inadequate shelters, and men struggled with lice and malnutrition. Dysentery and lethargy prevailed, and tensions escalated. The day arrived when the prisoners left Benghazi, heading to the port—a symbolic departure from one hardship to an uncertain fate.

CHAPTER 8

THE NINO BIXIO

Len's maritime journey to captivity unfolded against the tumultuous backdrop of war's tormented waters. A vessel named Nino Bixio, burdened with the weight of human suffering, served as the conduit for his passage to captivity in Italy. Packed tightly into the holds of the cargo vessel, almost 3000 prisoners of war, including over 160 New Zealanders, found themselves with no room to move.

The intended route typically led from Benghazi to Piraeus, through the Corinth Canal to Patras, and finally across the Adriatic to Taranto, Italy. However, fate took a cruel turn when the ship, en route with prisoners of war, became a target. Torpedoed by the British submarine HMS Turbulent, the Nino Bixio suffered the impact of two torpedoes, causing chaos in the tightly packed forward hold.

The Nino Bixio Transport Ship. © nzhistory.govt.nz.

Tragedy unfolded as an estimated 200 men lost their lives, and another 60 suffered injuries in the aftermath of the explosion. Amid panic and confusion, some prisoners jumped overboard, facing immediate drowning or drifting on makeshift rafts for weeks without food or water. Survivors, hauled up on deck by rope, faced extensive damage to the ship.

Despite the severe blow, the Nino Bixio managed to stay afloat. Towed by an escorting destroyer to Navarino in southern Greece, the dead were laid to rest, and the surviving POWs were transferred ashore. Those fit enough were eventually shipped to Southern Italy after a brief stop in Corinth.

Upon reaching the shores of Italy, the condition of most prisoners of war was pitiful. Many had endured months of deprivation in North Africa, facing limited supplies around Tobruk and El Alamein. Captured POWs had gone without sufficient food and drink for over two weeks, and personal hygiene had become a distant luxury. The arriving POWs were met with jeers and missiles from hostile locals, and occasionally met with retaliation from the aggrieved ANZAC.

Shaved heads, hot showers, and fumigated clothing awaited the prisoners at a large naval barracks. The process, though efficiently carried out, could not mask the appalling spectacle of lice-ridden, emaciated men draped in torn and greasy rags. Rations were finally issued, and the men were ferried across the harbour to a waiting train.

Marching into Campo PG75 at Bari, one of the main transit camps for British prisoners from North Africa, the men encountered further challenges. Many hadn't fully recovered from dysentery and other ailments contracted in North African transit camps. Lengthy periods on short rations had weakened them, resulting in widespread lethargy and cases of fainting during roll-call parades. Live infestations were common due to inadequate delousing arrangements, and a water shortage led to stagnant latrines.

With minimal books and makeshift recreation, Bari camp garnered few praises from those who endured the challenging summer of 1942. After a long, cold, and squalid journey, Len Hutchinson eventually arrived at P.G. 57, just outside the northern Italian city of Udine.

Len's arrival at P.G. 57 marked the beginning of a new chapter in his wartime odyssey. The challenges he faced in this camp would go beyond the physical toll of war; they would test the very core of who he thought he was. Life within the confines of P.G. 57 would become a crucible, forging Len Hutchinson into a man whose resilience and strength would be tempered by the fires of adversity. Little did he know that the experiences awaiting him in this northern Italian camp would etch indelible marks on his character, shaping the course of his journey through the turbulent landscape of World War II.

CHAPTER 9

CAMPO 57

The gates of Campo 57, rusted and weary, groaned as they swung open in Udine, Italy, unveiling a landscape scarred by the desolation of war. Len Hutchinson and his fellow prisoners stepped into a realm defined by barbed wire and vigilant watchtowers, their freedom now relegated to the confines of captivity. Campo 57, a name resonating in the history of wartime internment, emerged as the crucible where Len's resilience would face its sternest test.

Rows of barracks and open spaces characterised the camp, harbouring a diverse array of prisoners hailing from every corner of the globe. United by the shared experience of captivity, these men grappled with the challenges of their new reality within Campo 57. The starkness of the surroundings, initially daunting, found its counterbalance in the indomitable spirit that flickered within the hearts of those confined within its borders.

The Main Gate, Campo 57. © Ferdinando Nadalutti.

Gruppignano, situated near Udine between the Adriatic and the Alps, stood as a confinement for numerous New Zealanders during wartime. The Italians adhered to the principles of the Geneva Convention, consolidating prisoners of war from the same nationality within a single camp. At its peak, Gruppignano accommodated nearly 2000 New Zealanders, embodying the policy of nationality-based internment.

These train journeys, a distinctive feature of the prisoners-of-war routine, unfolded with varying levels of comfort. In cases where a large number of men travelled together, they often found themselves tightly packed into enclosed trucks resembling furniture vans, sometimes equipped with wooden seats and sometimes not. During halts along the journey, the guards were cautious about allowing prisoners out, even if the travel spanned three days. Conversely, smaller groups of prisoners travelling separately with their guards experienced comparatively better treatment. Some guards went the extra mile, using their own funds to purchase food and wine for the prisoners. Moreover, civilian travellers, irrespective of gender, were routinely displaced from their seats to accommodate the prisoners.

In each prisoner-of-war camp across Italy, a contingent of Carabinieri Reali, a police force renowned for its expertise predating the era of fascism, played a crucial role. Tasked with security, these men wielded significant authority, often capable of overruling even the Army commandant of the camps, regardless of their rank. They conducted thorough and unexpected searches of personal belongings, occasionally resorting to brutal treatment, presumably shaped by their dealings with civilian offenders.

At Gruppignano, the commanding officer was a colonel in the Carabinieri Reali, also serving as the military governor of Udine and an ardent Fascist, Colonel Calcaterra. Proud of the strictness of his discipline, the thirty cells at Gruppignano were consistently occupied. Despite his demise at the hands of Italian partisans, there was a semblance of respect for this authoritative figure among many prisoners. One account even expressed satisfaction that, unlike many Fascists during the fall of Mussolini, Calcaterra did not attempt to change allegiances.

The camp witnessed atrocities, including the shooting of a man who had gotten drunk while being assisted back to his hut by a carabiniere, and another shot while gathering wood after dark. Discipline, in general, was marked by petty measures and pin-pricking, with individuals whose faces twitched during roll-call parades swiftly dispatched to the cells without trial or inquiry. Excessive noise at night in any hut led to random selections by the Carabinieri, resulting in several men being thrown into cells.

Life within the camp's cells, while not ideal, had certain mitigating factors. Friends managed to smuggle in extra food and cigarettes, often concealed within ration bread. Collective punishments were imposed on the entire camp in the event of escapes. Despite the strict rule by the Carabinieri, Gruppignano earned favour among many prisoners for its efficient administration and the suppression of illicit activities that thrived in other camps.

Maximum camp strength at any one time was 5,500 and, from the end of 1942, comprised approximately a third each of Australians, New Zealanders and other nations (South Africa, India, UK, Canada, Cyprus, Palestine and Yugoslavia).

Upon their arrival at Gruppignano, having endured weeks or even months in transit camps, many men found themselves clad in mere rags and tatters. Both the men and their worn-out garments underwent a thorough disinfection process, and they were then outfitted with old Yugoslav or Greek uniforms. The eventual arrival of British uniforms through the Red Cross, along with woollen underwear in the first parcel from New Zealand House, brought immense relief.

In the camp, access to baths was sporadic, and lice infestations were commonplace. Even the periodic steaming of clothes failed to eradicate the problem entirely. The medical department lagged in terms of facilities and care, though conditions improved when an Australian medical officer assumed responsibility for sick parades. Prisoners had to resort to improvisation for their medical needs, grappling with ailments like the "57 twins," pneumonia, and kidney disease.

Delousing, Campo 57. © M.Lee Hill.

Under Calcaterra's regime, the camp descended into what could only be described as "a mass of neurosis," as the looming uncertainty of who would be victimised next cast a pervasive unease over the prisoners. The persistent fear of arbitrary punishment underscored the challenges of daily life within the confines of Gruppignano.

The huts in Gruppignano were elongated and confined, accommodating a staggering 96 men. Sleeping quarters were cramped, with double-tiered wooden bunks arranged in two rows down the centre of the hut. Each block of eight bunks was separated by a mere 18 inches, and a two-foot-wide passageway created a narrow aisle between the bunks and the walls. At both ends of the hut, a clear space of six feet was designated, and another space surrounded the solitary stove in each hut. This stove, however, offered the sole means of heating during the harsh winter months, and the provided wood allowance was woefully insufficient.

Constructed predominantly of wood and lined with the same material, the huts featured outer roofs made of rubberoid over wood. Unfortunately, the layout provided no space for essential activities such as reading, writing, or eating, forcing the occupants to perform these functions either on their bunks or outside in the open. Despite the initial construction of four recreation huts in 1942, they were swiftly repurposed for additional accommodations after only a few weeks of use. In this modified setup, 250 men were crammed into each hut, arranged in three-tiered bunks, further accentuating the challenges of living within the camp's confines.

Within the confines of Gruppignano, the available space for physical activity was generous. The prisoners engaged in a variety of sports such as cricket, football, baseball, volleyball, and deck tennis. Despite challenges, much of the sporting equipment was sourced from the British Red Cross, often indirectly. Interestingly, the Italian authorities prohibited the provision of cricket and baseball balls, prompting the resourceful prisoners to fashion their own using the string from Red Cross parcels.

A distinctive feature of life in this camp, as in many others, was the presence of 'blowers'—camp cookers. Given the severe scarcity of fuel throughout Italy, the prisoners showcased remarkable ingenuity in perfecting these cookers. Competitions were organised, pitting different types and operators against each other to determine the fastest time to boil water. Some 'blowers' could achieve the feat in less than two minutes, with several capable of bringing over a litre (approximately 1¾ pints) to a boil in record time. Surprisingly, even the Italian commandant took pride in displaying the camp's innovative cookers to visiting Generals.

There were fully functioning kitchens, only because of the enthusiasm and care of the POW staff.

The Cookhouse, Campo 57. © Ferdinando Nadalutti.

The infirmary was a wooden hut subdivided into two small storerooms, a dressing room and a ward. Later, another hut was added, containing two wards and an orderly's room. Also, a small dental unit was built.

Nestled in Gruppignano, the camp offered a stunning panorama with the Dolomite Mountains as a distant backdrop. Nature's beauty, echoed by ancient church bells, painted a timeless scene. Winters brought challenges, with frozen mud underfoot and the rhythmic stamping of feet to combat the cold. The camp, surrounded by nature's grandeur, transformed into a theatre where the elements dictated daily life.

Within the box-like huts, adorned with patterns on the walls, residents sought refuge. The strange scent of a charcoal burner wafted through the air, embedding itself in memories. Funeral processions added a sombre note, marking a symbolic journey beyond the camp's confines. Long waits for meals, the dance of searchlights, and the camaraderie amid scarcity defined the daily rhythm.

Gruppignano's beauty, echoing bells, and winter challenges wove a tapestry of memories. The majestic Alps, the rituals of life and death, and the resilience amid adversity became integral parts of Campo 57's collective narrative. The camp, with its breathtaking surroundings, encapsulated the indomitable spirit of those who called it home.

It was only during this time that Lieutenant Ken Macdonald wrote a letter to Len's mother back in New Zealand, informing her that Len was no longer classified as missing and was indeed a prisoner of war. Lieutenant Macdonald had known Len well back in Maadi Camp, where Len acted as the Lieutenant's batman. In the New Zealand division, batmen are treated more like friends, and Lieutenant Macdonald was able to help Len with extra leave and fewer parades. He also noted that he had not been so well taken care of since he had left home. It gave a smile to the face of May, and indeed Len's wife Norma, to know that Len had been a diligent and helpful valet to the officer.

Sometime during Len and Fred's time together in Campo 57, Len's wife Norma had sent over a family photo of herself and her sisters. Fred and almost all the men in the barracks knew each other's families as if they were their own, with Len explaining who all the sisters were and which ones were 'taken.' Fred pointed to one of them and declared, "I like the look of that one – save her for me when we get back to New Zealand!"

Len and Fred went on to have many more experiences and changes in camps, their friendship always enduring and remaining close.

Back row: far left is Len, centre is Fred.
© Family Archives.

During this time, young English folk were encouraged to write letters to single POWs, and so Fred struck up a pen pal friendship with Beryl Brown of South London.

Amidst internment, Len found solace in unexpected places. One notable endeavour that would leave an enduring mark on Campo 57 was the construction of a Catholic church. A symbol of faith and defiance against the oppression of captivity, the church stood as a testament to the resilience of the human spirit even in the darkest of times.

Len, along with fellow prisoners, dedicated themselves to the construction project. With meagre resources and improvised tools, they transformed the barren soil into a place of worship. The construction of the church became a communal effort, a manifestation of the unity that emerged in the face of adversity. Brick by brick, the church rose from the ground, a symbol of hope and a sanctuary for those seeking solace amid the harsh realities of war.

Amid the labour and hardships, Len forged friendships that would endure beyond the confines of Campo 57. One such bond, significant in Len's story, was with a man named Fred. The camaraderie between Len and Fred transcended the boundaries of nationality and circumstance. In the crucible of captivity, their friendship flourished, providing a source of strength and support in a world fraught with uncertainty.

Fred, a giant of a man with a heart to match, became more than a friend to Len; he became a brother in arms, a companion in the struggle for survival. Together, they navigated the challenges of internment, finding moments of respite in shared laughter and the simple pleasures that could be salvaged from the monotony of camp life.

The completion of the Catholic church marked not only a physical structure within Campo 57 but also a testament to the resilience and creativity of the human spirit in the face of oppression. The echoes of prayers and hymns within its walls became a rallying cry for hope, a reminder that even within the confines of captivity, the indomitable human spirit could transcend the boundaries of circumstance.

As Len Hutchinson continued his life within the wire fences of Campo 57, the bonds formed in the crucible of internment became threads woven into the fabric of his wartime experience. The church, standing tall amid the barracks, and the friendships forged, particularly with Fred, were beacons of light in the shadowy landscape of captivity. In the heart of Udine, Italy, Campo 57 became more than a prison—it became a canvas upon which the resilience, camaraderie, and unyielding spirit of men like Len Hutchinson were painted against the backdrop of war's darkest hours.

CHAPTER 10

THE CHURCH

The camp Chaplain, Father Giovani Cotta, part of the military administration, who before arriving at Campo 57 in Premaricacco, had already served in the prison camp in Prato Island, Balzano. He was already quite elderly but very active physically and mentally, friendly and chatty, even in English.

At times, he was permitted to give talks on non-military subjects, his favourites being Agriculture and Architecture, there being no lack of examples in Italy!

Supporting him in his project of building a church was Father Tom Lynch, a priest from Southampton and a captain in the British Army, and the New Zealander Ambrose Loughan, who later became a Dominican priest in 1951.

33517 - THE UNTOLD STORY OF PRIVATE F. L. HUTCHINSON

The easiest thing to find was labour, and so, what for many had seemed a dream, became a reality.

Once the location had been decided upon, the foundations were laid at the beginning of 1942 (before Len's internment), thanks to the help of numerous volunteers, mainly Australians and New Zealanders of the Catholic faith. Their labour was rewarded, according to memory and some surviving written fragments, by an increase in their daily allowance of bread.

Groups of 8-10 prisoners under armed guard were sent to the banks of the Natisone River to gather the stones needed for the building. Some tried to escape, unsuccessfully, but having overcome the difficult moments caused by these attempts, work slowly resumed on the church.

With the help of many willing hearts and hands, the building began to take shape. A rectangular nave made of stone and cement, the apse and a small presbytery. On the long sides were four windows with frames on the outside, and the front part was formed by a portico with a semi-circular colonnade, with stone supports and wooden beams holding up the roof, made of terracotta tiles. The altar and the entrance steps were prefabricated outside the camp. They were so precise in their construction that when the time came for them to be put in place, everything fitted together perfectly.

The building work was progressing rapidly, and soon, it was time to find a place for the wooden crucifix bought by the prisoners with their savings. According to some in-depth research by Mario Coccolo, the crucifix was carved in the studio of Senoner Holzbildhauer of Ortisei and painted by Corrado Pitscheider, also of Ortisei. Since the end of the war, it had been in safe safekeeping of the parish church of Premaricacco.

Dedicated to 'Our Lord Jesus Crucified', the new chapel so dear to Father Cotta and his team, witnessed its first and only Mass on 13 September 1943, only a week before the camp was evacuated by the Germans.

The Catholic Church built by the POWs. © Ferdinando Nadalutti.

CHAPTER 11

INTO THE DARK

In September 1943, Italy signed an armistice with Great Britain. A subsequent lack of action regarding the Italian prisoner-of-war camp by the British High Command then allowed the Germans to empty most of them and transport their inhabitants north into German-occupied territory. Len was transported first to Stalag VIIIA, then six months later, in May 1944, to Stalag VIIIB/344. Both were located in what is now Poland.

From those camps that were taken over by German troops in September 1943, all except the few who succeeded in hiding were marched to the nearest railway station. The Germans took what precautions they could to prevent escapes - a strong guard along the route, threats before setting out of the dire consequences that would follow any attempted breaks, even a demonstration with a flame-thrower at Campo PG 57. The weather was at its hottest, and men struggled along in the dust, wearing or carrying whatever possessions they could, at the pace set by the guards. Some dropped with exhaustion from the heat and the exertion and were brought along later by truck. The guarding was efficient, and there was little chance of breaking away.

Most of the trains went north via Verona, through the Brenner Pass to Innsbruck, though a few took the more easterly Tarvisio Pass to Villach. They were almost entirely made up of cattle trucks and closed goods wagons with very few third-class carriages, some of them Italian rolling stock commandeered by the German military authorities, others returning north after having brought German troops and equipment south for the Italian campaign. Into these trucks the prisoners were packed, as many as fifty in each, though the number was reduced for officers to about thirty-five. With thirty-five, it was almost impossible for everyone to lie down at once, and with fifty, for everyone to sit down, even when kits had been hung on the sides and from the roof beams. The sliding doors were closed and bolted, and prisoners were left for the journey with at most two small openings in the sides of the truck for air and light, no provision for latrines, and only such food and water as they had been able to carry with them. Though most had ample Red Cross food, it did not take long for men perspiring in the 'oven-like heat' to empty their water bottles, and for those with any kind of dysentery, the journey was a miserable experience. There were occasional halts on the journey north, often not long enough for every truckload to be allowed out. On the longer journeys, there were considerable halts at stations and sometimes meals from the German Red Cross.

From the moment they were locked inside, men in almost every truck looked about for ways out of it. Before the train bringing those from Campo PG 57 had reached the junction at Udine, some had crawled through the small windows and jumped clear, and from Udine onwards, the stream of escapers continued. There were similar losses from the first trains on the main line north to the Brenner Pass. In later trains, those openings that were not barred were closed with barbed wire to prevent such escapes.

Transporting the POWs in cattle trucks, Italy. © M.Lee Hill.

Nevertheless, in some of the wooden trucks, a hole was made near the bolt securing one of the sliding doors. A hand was put through, and the door opened, leaving the whole truckload free to make a break, and several truckloads did.

For most of the prisoners, the journey was one of acute discomfort and, for some, of real physical hardship. But it was relieved by glimpses of splendid alpine scenery, which led at least one prisoner to call the Austrian Tyrol 'the most beautiful country I have seen since leaving my own'. There was interest in the difference of landscape and dwellings from those in Italy; interest too in calling out to groups of British prisoners working alongside the railway, some of whom had been in German hands since the end of the campaign in France.

Those from Campo 57 were the first large party from Italy to reach Stalag XVIIIC at Markt Pongau in Austria, a transit camp which then held some 1000 prisoners of several other European nationalities. Though in a beautiful alpine setting on the left bank of the Salzach, roughly 25 miles south of Salzburg, the camp was very dirty, and the barracks were infested with vermin. Many prisoners, to avoid the bedbugs, preferred to sleep on the floor wrapped in their great-coats; a number would have had to in any case, as there were not enough beds to go round, nor any blankets. For the first time, they tasted the typical German stalag fare - vegetable soup and 'black' bread, boiled potatoes and mint tea. There, too, they went through the registration, searching, and delousing routine already described elsewhere, but had all their spare clothing, boots, and blankets confiscated. After a fortnight or so, most went north to Stalag VIIIA at Görlitz in Saxony, miles east of Dresden. Several thousand British and American prisoners passed through this camp, and by mid-November, only 450-odd remained.

CHAPTER 12

POLISH CAMP AND MINES

The winds of change swept through Len Hutchinson's journey of captivity as he, along with a contingent of prisoners from Campo 57, found himself on the move once again. The destination: Stalag 8A, a name that would resonate with hardship and endurance.

Stalag 8A or VIIIA – Gorlitz was a German prisoner of war camp located just south of the town of Gorlitz in Lower Silesia, east of the river Neisse. The camp's location lies in today's Polish town of Zgorzelec, just over the river from Gorlitz. It was initially set up as a Hitler Jugend (Hitler Youth) camp, converted in October 1939 to house Polish prisoners, and later held up to 30,000 Allied prisoners before the Germans began evacuating it in February 1945 (The Long March). On 14 February 1945, the American and British prisoners were marched out of the camp westward in advance of the Soviet offensive into Germany. The evacuation process was carried out gradually until May 1945. The evacuation took place on foot, with all means of transport driving in front of the people for military purposes. Some of those evacuated were taken to Bavaria, the others to Thuringia, where they were freed by Allied forces. The last evacuation of the camp took place on 7 May 1945, when the Soviet army released the remaining prisoners.

Stalag 8A. © Wikipedia.

The camp covered over 70 acres of sloping countryside on the eastern outskirts of the town of Görlitz. One of the oldest prisoner-of-war camps in Germany, it had barracks of the same type as those at Lamsdorf and had held prisoners of several Allied European countries. When New Zealand men arrived from Italy, they contained French, Belgians and Serbs, together with several Russians, in an adjacent but carefully segregated compound. The portion of the camp allotted to the newcomers was in bad repair, with many missing doors and windows and a bad shortage of beds and palliasses. It was also infested with lice and bedbugs, and though the former were soon overcome, the latter persisted. There was a very poor water supply and the usual rather primitive latrine system. But under good leadership, the camp soon began to show improvement. Generous gifts of food and tobacco from the French and Belgians tided the British prisoners over a lean period until copious Red Cross supplies of all kinds began to arrive in October. In time, it became possible to organise all the amenities common in other, longer-established British camp communities.

The stalag very quickly became overcrowded and remained so until sufficient working parties were moved out to work camps. All those below the rank of corporal underwent a rather cursory medical examination by a German doctor and were graded according to the heaviness of the work he considered they were fit to undertake. Before the end of the year, hundreds of men had gone to work in coal mines or stone quarries, at sugar, glass or paper factories, on railway construction or other building work in Arbeitskommandos attached to Stalag VIIIA.

33517 - THE UNTOLD STORY OF PRIVATE F. L. HUTCHINSON

As many as could be got out to work were sent to coal mines, sugar-beet factories, aerodrome construction jobs, and other work in the neighbourhood. Without Red Cross food parcels and camp concerts, boxing tournaments and other sports, this unpleasant existence would have been hard to bear. Boils, a common complaint among prisoners of war, became particularly prevalent. Sickness gave several an opportunity to get back to Stalag, though many others who were sick were ordered out to work by the German doctor or the commandant, whose decision as to whether a prisoner was fit enough to work was final.

The transition from the relative freedom of Campo 57 to the confines of Stalag 8A marked a shift in Len's captivity. The prisoners, now accustomed to the camaraderie and collective efforts of the Italian camp, faced the stark reality of forced labour in the Polish mines. The once-familiar routines of construction and shared endeavours were replaced by gruelling days spent toiling underground, the echoes of pickaxes against rock reverberating through the tunnels.

Conditions in Stalag 8A were harsh, the camp a stark reminder of the dehumanising nature of war. The barracks, crowded and often infested with vermin, became the only respite from the physical demands of forced labour. The prisoners, clad in threadbare uniforms and weathered boots, endured the biting cold of Polish winters and the oppressive heat of summers, their bodies pushed to the limits of resilience.

Amidst the hardships, the resilience of the prisoners shone through. The indomitable spirit that had fuelled the construction of the Catholic Church in Campo 57 now manifested in the shared determination to endure the tribulations of Stalag 8A. The camaraderie among the prisoners, forged in the crucible of adversity, became a source of strength. Shared laughter in the face of despair, whispered words of encouragement, and the unwavering support of comrades formed a shield against the dehumanising effects of captivity.

The forced labour in the Polish mines, a relentless cycle of toil and fatigue, tested the physical and mental fortitude of Len and his fellow prisoners. Yet, within the confines of hardship, bonds deepened, and a collective resolve emerged. The tunnels, dimly lit and echoing with the sounds of labour, became a symbol of the prisoners' resilience—a testament to their ability to find light even in the darkest recesses of captivity.

Hours of actual work at the mine were long; usually eight and a half hours in the coal seam, preparations beforehand and cleaning up afterwards, added another hour or two, and for a long time, only one Sunday in four was a free day. This was later the subject of an official complaint when the International Red Cross Committee investigated all the German mining camps. Falls of stone and coal caused crushed and broken bones, and there were many cases of 'gassing' below the ground during work. Down in the mine, prisoners were employed in pushing or shovel-loading trucks, working alongside Polish men and boys, sometimes ankle-deep in water. Above the surface, they worked with Polish women 'separating', loading scrap iron, coal and rations, and doing camp fatigues.

There was much threatening with pistols by both Polish-born overseers and German guards to keep the prisoners working. But constant bullying of this kind failed to make much impression on men who by this time had several years of prisoner-of-war experience behind them, had been screamed at by guards, snarled at by Alsatian police dogs, and threatened with firearms too often to be worried. They shovelled the required minimum of wagon loads, less if they could deceive the overseer, and quickly learnt all they could loaf on the job and get away with it.

Among men working under such conditions and on various shifts throughout the whole day and night, it was unlikely that artistic and intellectual recreations would flourish as they did in other camps. There were almost no facilities for reading, and even letters were short in mid-1944. Football and boxing matches held on the rare free days and an occasional concert were the only light relief from the weariness and monotony of a life of continual dirt, hunger and oppression.

CHAPTER 13

STALAG 8B/344

Stalag 8B/VIIIB Lamsdorf stood as the largest Stalag in the Third Reich, hosting tens of thousands of prisoners, predominantly Russian. Amid its expansive grounds, a smaller camp accommodated approximately 16,000 POWs from Britain, Australia, Canada, India, New Zealand, and South Africa. Adding to the complexity, by the close of 1943, Lamsdorf underwent a redesignation as Stalag 344, while a sub-camp in Teschen, 125 km southeast, assumed the mantle of the new Stalag VIIIB.

The camp received trainloads of men directly bound for Stalag VIIIB, along with others relocated from Stalag VIIIA. This transformation ballooned the already massive camp, which had shown signs of improvement with a new German commandant. The population swelled to well over

30,000, with 10,000 within the stalag itself. Sleeping arrangements became makeshift, with men finding repose on tables, forms, or simply the floor. The overcrowding extended to various camp services, amplifying the challenges faced by those confined within its sprawling confines.

In Stalag 8B/VIIIB Lamsdorf, men hailing from Italian camps found themselves reunited with old comrades from the campaigns in Greece and Crete. Their arrival sparked reflections on the disparities in discipline within this camp compared to their experiences in Italy, particularly in Campo PG 57. The atmosphere seemed to foster clandestine activities unknown to the enemy. Observers witnessed the curious spectacle of shackling, with handcuffs issued but not enforced, and encountered individuals living in the camp whose records were either nonexistent or falsified.

The camp also harboured challenges, notably from a group attempting to exploit fellow prisoners through intimidation, brandishing blade-razors in their bid to improve their own conditions. Meanwhile, newcomers, already assessed by German doctors for their fitness for specific labour types, eventually departed for assignments in coal mines and other workplaces in Silesia.

In December, faced with the challenge of overcrowding in Lamsdorf, German authorities implemented administrative solutions. Staff members were reassigned to establish new base camps at Teschen and Sagan, which were subsequently designated Stalag VIIIB and Stalag VIIIC. Concurrently, the original Lamsdorf camp underwent renumbering, now identified as Stalag 344. To streamline the organisation of the Silesian working camps, they were strategically distributed among Stalag 344 and Stalags VIIIA, B, and C.

The population at Stalag VIIIB in Teschen swiftly grew to 11,000 British Commonwealth prisoners, with nearly 1,000 New Zealanders among them. However, only a small proportion of this total resided at the base camp, while the majority engaged in labour across more than fifty Arbeitskommandos throughout the region.

The prisoners of war worked as labourers for the Polish men working in the mines. The prisoners did the hardest tasks, and conditions were not pleasant - the mines were damp and wet, and there was water everywhere. Each man was issued with an ID tag and a carbide lamp every time he went down into the mine. The lamp had a flint on it so that it could be lit, and it made a gas that burned when water from the mine dripped onto the lamp.

Three daily shifts, each spanning approximately 8 hours, structured the laborious routine: from 6 am to 2 pm, 2 pm to 10 pm, and the night shift lasting from 10 pm until 6 am the following morning. The morning and afternoon shifts focused on coal extraction, while the evening shift involved relocating equipment and arranging supports for the forthcoming day's tasks. A subset of workers toiled during the night, handling the movement of equipment and installing new support structures—a challenging and perilous undertaking.

Prisoners thought about trying to sabotage the mine, but there were always men working on the lowest levels, so any attempt would inevitably endanger many prisoners. On occasion, the lift was damaged, and men in lower levels had to escape by a complex system of ladders, but nothing more extensive was done because the resultant loss of life would have been great.

The men lived in huts beside the mine. There were 10 to 12 men in each hut; men on different shifts were billeted together, which made it very difficult to get any real sleep. The food was the same as at the other camps - bread and coffee for breakfast and one meal a day of soup. Thankfully, the men were still able to receive their Red Cross Parcels; without them, they would not have survived.

Here's an excerpt from one POW: "In the bitter cold of Silesia, we were assigned to work in the coal mines. I vividly recall my first task—keeping the conveyor belts moving smoothly at the junction of two conveyor belts. The pit props, arranged in a cross-section, added an element of fear as they creaked sporadically. Every sound, every movement in that underground labyrinth sent shivers down my spine. But amidst the uncertainty, moments of camaraderie and unexpected kindness emerged.

Assigned to load steel pit props onto a trolley with a fellow prisoner, we navigated the dark tunnels. An unexpected event during a blasting operation plunged me into darkness, with only the distant light from my companion's lamp guiding me. It was a surreal experience, feeling my way through the blackness hundreds of feet below ground.

A Polish colleague, Anteg, became an unlikely ally during our treacherous exploration of pitfalls. His caution, ensuring the safety of each seam before entry, demonstrated the bonds formed in adversity. In a quiet exchange, I shared a bar of Cadbury's milk chocolate with him, a small gesture that bridged language and cultural gaps.

Life on the pit top offered moments of respite, with a generous girl occasionally dropping sandwiches into our coal trucks. Amidst the hardship, these acts of kindness became beacons of humanity in a world filled with uncertainty.

As January arrived, our routine abruptly ended. The Germans, armed with rifles, barged into our lives at six in the morning, signalling the beginning of what would later be known as the death march. A month-long journey through the harsh Eastern European winter awaited us. We strolled—or rather, stumbled—through the snow-covered landscapes, facing the constant threat of frostbite and hunger. The death toll mounted, especially among the Russians, as the march became a harrowing test of endurance.

The march, characterised by makeshift shelter in barns and snow-covered sleep in the open, pushed us to the limits of physical and mental resilience. The scarcity of food made even frozen runner beans a sought-after delicacy. Frostbite began to gnaw at my toes, prompting me to fall out temporarily. In a barn acting as a makeshift hospital, I clung to a daily ration of bread and a bit of butter, relying on the fortitude instilled by thoughts of home.

Frostbitten toes and a compromised immune system marked my journey to Nuremberg, where dysentery struck with a vengeance. The American guns in the distance hinted at liberation drawing near. The arrival of Sherman tanks and the jubilant shout, "The Yanks are here!" marked the end of our ordeal. The subsequent chaos, as liberated prisoners gorged on Compo packs, added a touch of irony to our newfound freedom.

Nuremberg Airport became a pivotal point, with Dakotas flying us back to Ostend. Marlene Dietrich's unexpected appearance brought a momentary diversion, a memory etched in time. From Ostend, we were deloused, given baths, and provided with clean clothes before embarking on a boat to Tilbury. The first hearty meal aboard the ship, thick stew with white bread and butter, marked a return to nourishment. The journey continued to Tilbury, then Haywards Heath for documentation, and finally, home."

This testimony, filled with the raw experiences of a POW, vividly captures the essence of survival, camaraderie, and the indomitable human spirit amidst the harshest of conditions. It serves as a poignant reminder of the shared trials endured by those who found themselves prisoners of war during tumultuous times. As we reflect on this account, it becomes evident that Len and Fred, and perhaps countless others, may have traversed similar paths of hardship, forming bonds and summoning resilience in the face of adversity. Their untold stories echo through the annals of history, testaments to the strength of the human spirit during the darkest chapters of the past.

CHAPTER 14

A SOLDIER'S STORY

"As I reflect on those challenging days of captivity, my mind takes me back to the bitter cold of Upper Silesia. It was November 5th, 1943, when we were herded into another closed cattle wagon at Stalag VIII A Gorlitz Mays and transported to a harsh new reality. For the next 14 months, this desolate place would be my 'home.'

Our first assignment at the Zabrzec commando involved working on railway sidings, where we often glimpsed young, dejected German soldiers headed for the horrors of the Russian front. Amidst this, my comrades and I seized the opportunity to 'lift' extra food from supply wagons right under the guards' noses. We became masters of diversion, engaging in snowball fights and building snowmen while helping ourselves to potatoes. Our clever ploys worked until the guards discovered peelings in one of the huts. Sabotage also became part of our repertoire, uncoupling wagons to disrupt supplies heading to the front.

In what seemed like a 'reward' for our audacious behaviour, we were dispatched to Kazimer on February 10th, 1944. There, we found ourselves loading coal underground in the Pecan and Saturn mines. The work was not only excruciatingly hard and dangerous but also took place in dreadful conditions—13-hour shifts, light failures, and rock slides were our daily challenges. However, amidst the hardship, I forged an unexpected friendship with August, a Polish mining engineer, who insisted I work with him in the disaster and rescue squad. Little did I know that I was stepping from the frying pan into the fire, for these Katowice/Gliwice mines would soon become the crucible of my hardest POW experiences.

In the dark tunnels, surrounded by the constant threat of rats, falling timbers, and rocks, I experienced some of the most harrowing moments of my life. Singing 'You Are My Sunshine' each night as we descended into the abyss became a ritual, a feeble attempt to keep our spirits up. Despite the exhaustion, we clung to fragments of normalcy, looking forward to occasional football matches, even against the guards. Working through Christmas without celebration, our 'gift' was half a horse's head shared among 400 prisoners—a thin soup that symbolised our meagre existence. My personal treat was wrapping my clothes for delousing around a can of condensed milk, turning it into a caramel-like delight.

Unbeknownst to us, just 20 miles away, the notorious Auschwitz death camp cast its ominous shadow. My resilience and ability to pull my weight were tested daily, while many of my friends were not as fortunate.

The Long March West marked a new chapter in our ordeal. After three days of walking and freezing train journeys, we left the Russian POWs behind and joined a British column. This initiated an 88-day, 800-mile trek through the Sudetenland, Czechoslovakia, and southeast Germany. With little food or shelter, our 250–300-man column was forced to march 10 to 15 miles a day, violating the Geneva Convention's maximum of 20km. The freezing conditions, coupled with hunger, frostbite, and exhaustion, made it a gruelling journey. Sleep came in barns, farmyards, and haystacks—wherever we could find refuge. The internet, in recent years, has allowed me to translate the old German place names and trace our route through modern Czech Republic maps.

The march brought its share of escape attempts, with the tale of Alf Forester convincing me to join a risky venture. A chance encounter with a Cambridge-educated German Major added a surreal touch to our narrative, underlining the unexpected human connections in the midst of chaos.

As the march continued, the dwindling resources and hardships became more pronounced. The revelation of our route through Czechoslovakia, translated and mapped in modern times, added a poignant layer of understanding.

33517 - THE UNTOLD STORY OF PRIVATE F. L. HUTCHINSON

The final leg of our march into Bavaria offered fleeting moments of respite and encounters with RAF planes. Liberation was on the horizon as American fighters dipped their wings overhead, signalling the imminent end of our captivity. The surreal transition to freedom included celebrating my third birthday as a POW.

Post-liberation, the narrative shifts to the joy of newfound freedom. Exploring Thiermietnach and surrounding areas, hearing the news of Hitler's demise, and the journey home evoked a mix of emotions. The white cliffs of the Seven Sisters emerge as a symbol of hope on the horizon.

Returning to civilian life proved challenging, marked by a lack of counselling and difficulties in readjusting. The abrupt shift from the rigours of captivity to everyday life underscored the broader struggles faced by returning POWs. My resilience, fueled by a love of sports, became a thread of hope amidst the ordeal. The testimony, once silenced, found a voice in later years, emphasising the importance of sharing these untold stories."

This testimony is shared to give an eyewitness account of what Len and Fred, along with their comrades, endured on the Long March.

CHAPTER 15

THE LONG MARCH

POWs who did not succeed in escaping could only await the end of the war for their liberation and repatriation. With Soviet victories during 1944 putting camps in eastern Germany and Poland under threat of being overrun, the German authorities determined to evacuate the POWs to the west. Later Allied successes in the West would force similar action in Western Germany.

For the POWs, these steps initiated a period of great trial. Some of the POWs were moved by train, but most were forced to evacuate their camps on foot. For POWs whose diet had long been inadequate, such exertion was an ordeal. It was made worse by atrocious weather during the winter of 1944–45. In the confusion of the march, food supply arrangements became haphazard. To add to the dangers, some of the POWs' guards, resentful of the obvious decline in their country's fortunes, took out their frustration on the men in their charge. A New Zealander was shot dead when he bent down to pick up bread thrown to him by compassionate civilians.

Some of these POW movements ended when the groups arrived at large camps in central Germany, which were eventually overrun by Allied forces. Others continued to move until the end, when their guards generally disappeared, and Allied units soon arrived. Those still in Eastern Europe were liberated by Soviet forces.

The frigid winds of Eastern Europe carried whispers of uncertainty as Len Hutchinson and his fellow prisoners, their bodies battered but spirits unbroken, embarked on a journey that would come to be known as the Long March. This gruelling odyssey, covering over 800 miles in freezing conditions, would test the limits of endurance, camaraderie, and the indomitable will to survive.

POWs marching through the wintry snow on The Long March.
© Canadian Battlefield Tours.

The Long March began as an ominous silhouette on the horizon; the prisoners of Stalag 8b/344 thrust into the harsh reality of relentless movement.

With only a few hours to prepare, the prisoners set off in early 1945 with packed blankets, warm clothing, as much Red Cross, and as many other food and personal items as they could carry. But many of the packs proved too heavy and cumbersome for the long marches through snow, and much gear was thrown by the wayside.

Almost every night, they were tightly packed into barns, which, though they afforded some shelter, were dark and cold. Men slept close together in pairs or in larger groups to make more efficient use of the available blankets and body warmth. The bitter cold of the winter air cut through their worn-out uniforms, and the snow-laden landscapes stretched endlessly before them.

Many of the guards, especially the older men, were in worse condition than the prisoners, and a number were left behind at various stages of the journey, unable to carry on.

Len, drawing on the resilience forged in previous chapters of his wartime journey, pressed forward. The biting cold seeped into his bones, and each step on the frozen ground felt like a battle against the elements. The physical toll of the Long March was compounded by the scarcity of provisions, with meagre rations barely sustaining the prisoners through the arduous trek.

Yet, within the crucible of adversity, bonds deepened among the marching prisoners. Len found himself side by side with his steadfast companion, Fred. The camaraderie that had blossomed in the confines of Campo 57 and endured the hardships of Stalag 8A, 8B/344, now faced its greatest test. Fred, the giant with a heart as resilient as his frame, became a pillar of support for Len, and together, they navigated the harsh realities of the Long March.

The days blurred into nights as the prisoners traversed the frozen landscapes, their breaths visible in the icy air. Each step was a testament to their endurance; each mile covered a triumph over the looming spectre of despair. The Long March became a crucible of shared suffering, where the collective will to survive forged bonds among the prisoners that transcended the physical and the temporal.

As the march continued, Len and his fellow prisoners faced not only the relentless cold but also the uncertainty of their destination. The Long March, orchestrated by the shifting dynamics of war, unfolded with an air of ambiguity, the prisoners driven forward by an unspoken understanding that their survival depended on the collective strength they found in each other.

In the face of adversity, Len Hutchinson's perseverance became a beacon of hope. The camaraderie among the marching prisoners, the whispered words of encouragement, and the shared burden of the Long March fostered a sense of unity that defied the dehumanising effects of captivity. The frozen landscapes, though harsh and unforgiving, became witness to the resilience of the human spirit—a spirit that found expression in the bonds formed during those arduous days and nights.

As the Long March neared its end, the prisoners, weary and weathered, emerged from the crucible of frozen landscapes with a tenacity that belied the physical toll. The bonds forged in the relentless march became a testament to the unbroken spirit of those who, against all odds, had traversed the freezing expanse—a spirit that would endure, leaving an indelible mark on Len Hutchinson's journey through the tumultuous landscapes of World War II.

As their journey broke in France or Belgium, the men spent a night, or at times, only a few hours, at a specially prepared transit centre before going on. Most of the men seem to have gone to either Rheims or Brussels.

The transit centre at Brussels, which was the one to which it had been intended that the majority of British ex-prisoners should go, received and sent on some 40,000 of them in three weeks at the end of April and in early May. As the streams of Dakotas arrived from Germany and unloaded trucks to the ex-prisoners at the transit centre, at the same time, streams of British four-engine bombers were taking on for England those who had already passed through. At the centre, they were given showers, new uniforms, and a pay advance. They could stay a night in a hotel run by the Belgian Red Cross Society; they had full use of recreation rooms run by the YMCA; and they could go on leave to take advantage of private hospitality or to buy presents in the city, or just to look around. A liaison officer speaks of the prisoners being 'all in rocketing good spirits'. But most of the men's spirits did not reach their climax until they arrived in England, for not until then were they back among people and in an environment nearly the same as their own. In England, there was the additional thrill of seeing again (or seeing for the first time) the country from which their forebears of most of them had come during the last hundred years. At this point, many who had consistently kept diaries finished abruptly. Here was an opportunity to be seized rather than written about, and most of the diarists no doubt had much the same feeling as the one whose last entry reads, "Can't be bothered writing anymore. Going to start out and enjoy myself."

CHAPTER 16

LIBERATION

A rrival at the destination after the Long March. The end of the war and the initial reactions of Len and his fellow prisoners.

The horizon, once a distant and unreachable line on the frozen landscape, finally drew near as Len Hutchinson and his fellow prisoners reached the end of their arduous Long March. The destination, still shrouded in the uncertainty of war, emerged as a haven from the relentless cold and a beacon of hope for the weary souls who had endured the crucible of the march.

As the prisoners approached their final stop, the air crackled with a mix of anticipation and weariness. The guards, now less imposing against the backdrop of a shifting war, guided the prisoners into a new chapter—one that hinted at liberation and the promise of a world free from the shackles of captivity.

The arrival at the destination marked not only the physical end of the Long March but also the beginning of a collective reckoning with the reality that the war was drawing to a close. The prisoners, their bodies worn and spirits tempered in the crucible of adversity, stood on the threshold of liberation.

The end of the war echoed through the landscape, heralded by distant sounds of celebration and the fading spectre of conflict. For Len Hutchinson and his fellow prisoners, the news of liberation carried with it a mixture of disbelief and elation. The war, which had defined their lives for years, was now unravelling, and the possibility of freedom loomed on the horizon.

As the news of liberation spread through the ranks of prisoners, an emotional tide swept through the captive souls. Tears of relief mingled with smiles of disbelief, and the realisation that the chains of captivity were finally loosening sank in. The Long March, a journey fraught with hardship, now stood as a testament to the prisoners' resilience in the face of the darkest hours of war.

The initial reactions of Len and his fellow prisoners to the news of liberation were varied—a spectrum of emotions ranging from euphoria to cautious optimism. The world beyond the wire fences, once distant and obscured, now beckoned with the promise of a life reclaimed. The possibility of reuniting with families, of returning to a world reshaped by the currents of history, filled the air with a sense of anticipation.

As the days unfolded, the reality of liberation took shape. The guards, once stern enforcers of captivity, receded into the background. The prisoners, now free to move beyond the confines of barbed wire, ventured into the landscapes that had been the backdrop to their captive existence. The war, with its echoes of gunfire and the distant rumble of conflict, began to fade into the annals of history.

Liberation, though a cause for celebration, also marked a period of adjustment for Len Hutchinson and his fellow prisoners. The transition from captivity to freedom brought with it the challenges of reacclimatizing to a world that had moved forward in their absence. The scars of war, both physical and emotional, lingered as reminders of the trials endured during the Long March and years of internment.

For Len and his comrades, liberation was not just a moment in time but a transformative experience that would shape the contours of their post-war lives. As they navigated the uncertain terrain of freedom, the echoes of the Long March and the resilience forged in captivity became guiding lights, leading them towards a future marked by the promise of a world beyond the wire fences—a world where the indomitable human spirit had triumphed over the darkest shadows of war.

REPATRIATION

A New Zealand repatriation unit was established in the United Kingdom under the command of Major-General Howard Kippenberger late in 1944. With its headquarters at Westgate in Kent, this unit had wings at Folkestone, Cliftonville and Broadstairs, and a hospital at Haine, to receive 2NZEF POWs, who were expected to arrive in orderly sequence from the continent. Separate arrangements were made for air force and naval POWs, with the former going to a camp at Brighton.

The first draft of about 500 POWs left for New Zealand at the end of May 1945, and by the end of August, more than 4000 were home.

The transition from the landscapes of captivity to the shores of the United Kingdom marked a pivotal chapter in

Len Hutchinson's post-war journey. The war-weary prisoners, including Len and his fellow comrades, found themselves aboard ships bound for recovery and reacclimatization in a land far from the echoes of conflict.

The journey across the sea, once a perilous passage, now carried a different weight—a sense of hope and anticipation for the men who had endured the hardships of war. As the shores of the United Kingdom came into view, the once-distant possibility of returning to normalcy became more tangible, and the horizon of freedom expanded beyond the confines of internment.

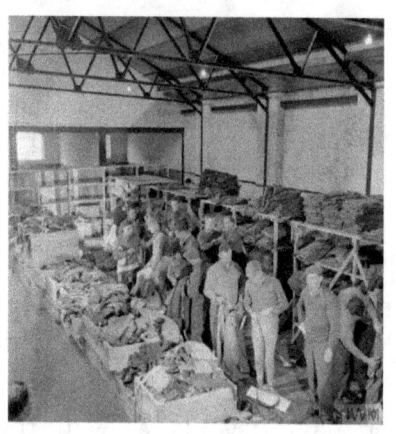

Arriving in the United Kingdom.
©*Ministry of Information, Photo Division, D-24518.*

Upon arrival, Len and his comrades were billeted in UK barracks, a stark contrast to the confines of the camps they had left behind. The barracks, though a far cry from they homes they had known before the war, represented a sanctuary for recovery and reacclimatisation. The transition from captivity to the barracks marked the beginning of a slow and deliberate process of returning to normalcy.

Life in the UK barracks was a delicate dance between the past and the present. The men, worn and weathered by the tribulations of war, faced the challenges of reintegration into a society that had moved forward in their absence. The camaraderie forged in the crucible of captivity provided a foundation, a support system that eased the burden of readjustment.

The slow process of returning to normalcy unfolded in the daily routines of the barracks. Medical care, counselling, and the shared experiences of recovery became the pillars on which the men leaned as they navigated the physical and psychological scars of war. The simple comforts of a warm bed, nourishing meals, and the freedom to move without the constraints of wire fences became poignant symbols of the journey from captivity to recovery.

The United Kingdom, though foreign, became a land of healing, a place where Len and his fellow prisoners could rediscover the rhythms of life beyond the shadow of war. The process of reacclimatisation, while challenging, unfolded against the backdrop of a nation that recognised the sacrifices made by those who had endured the crucible of conflict.

*Soldiers arriving at the barracks, United Kingdom.
©Ministry of Information, Photo Division, D-24508.*

As the days turned into weeks and the weeks into months, the men in the UK barracks began to rebuild their lives. Friendships, forged in the crucible of war, endured in the barracks as the shared experiences of recovery became the threads that bound them together. The scars of captivity, though etched into their bodies and minds, became markers of resilience rather than symbols of defeat.

For Len Hutchinson, the transfer to the UK represented not only a physical journey from captivity but also a metaphorical passage from the shadows of war to the dawning light of freedom. The barracks, though temporary, provided a sanctuary for healing and reflection—a space where the men could begin to reconcile the complexities of their wartime experiences with the promise of a future beyond the barracks walls.

In retrospect, there were initial discussions about repatriating New Zealand prisoners of war (POWs) through Italy and Egypt, but practical considerations led to their evacuation to Britain. This decision was widely embraced by many New Zealand POWs, who saw it as an opportunity to complete studies, undergo examinations, gain specialised knowledge or experience in their respective occupations, reunite with family members, and temporarily rejoin their wives and children residing there. As the war in Europe concluded, the prisoners were transferred to transport hubs and subsequently moved to Britain.

Anticipating a return to a familiar environment, the men's initial apprehensions were rooted in the struggle with their identity as defeated soldiers. Upon arrival in Britain, some POWs expressed surprise at the warm welcome extended to them. The rigid confines of captivity and the infrequent contact with the outside world had tempered their expectations. As recounted by one of the returning officers, they felt a sense of guilt about being prisoners and were astonished to find a welcoming reception in Britain.

The reception at rehabilitation centres, marked by small acts of hospitality, left a lasting impression on the returning soldiers. Staff Sergeant John Hobbs highlighted the significance of simple gestures, such as being greeted by a smiling W.A.A.F. girl and an R.A.F. boy. These acts of kindness made them feel like heroes, a stark contrast to their expectations. Warrant Officer Galbraith Hyde emphasised the emotional impact of such gestures, expressing gratitude for the opportunity to shower at leisure and experience a clean environment after years of captivity.

The positive reception at rehabilitation centres, though initially confusing for some, helped dispel the prisoners' concerns about returning home. Despite the stigma associated with captivity, the returning New Zealanders often remarked on the warmth of their welcome. Food played a crucial role in shaping their expectations, with memories of scarce rations in captivity contrasted with the freedom to choose meals at the rehabilitation centres.

Preparations for accommodating the approximately 8000 New Zealand POWs in Britain began in March 1944, with housing proving challenging to secure. Despite setbacks, properties in Folkestone, Margate, and Westgate were requisitioned, many of which were seaside hotels before the war. These locations prioritised the rehabilitation of the men as civilians rather than military reintegration.

In March 1944, preparations commenced for accommodating the approximately 8000 New Zealand POWs in Britain. While the initial plan was to establish the repatriation headquarters at Dover, logistical constraints led to a last-minute change, redirecting efforts to create rest centres in Folkestone, Margate, and Westgate. These locations,

33517 - THE UNTOLD STORY OF PRIVATE F. L. HUTCHINSON

once seaside hotels, were deemed more suitable for the envisioned rehabilitation of the POWs as civilians.

The emphasis on treating the returning soldiers as civilians awaiting transport home was evident in the measures taken at these camps. Staff Sergeant John Hobbs expressed gratitude for the minimal discipline imposed and the assurance that they would be regarded as civilians awaiting discharge from the forces after three months of leave. The goal was to make the POWs feel at home, facilitate their physical and mental recovery, and provide opportunities for leisure, including hospitality in private homes.

Hobbs emphasised the deliberate effort to avoid turning the rehabilitation centre into another form of prison. The men were treated as civilians, not captives or soldiers, underscoring the importance of helping them forget the hardships of captivity and restoring their physical and mental well-being.

The significance of these encounters lay in the opportunity they provided for the returning soldiers to fully immerse themselves in civilian life again. A pivotal aspect of their rehabilitation was the reconnection with loved ones in New Zealand. Throughout their captivity, intermittent correspondence with home served as one of the few ways for POWs to maintain a sense of continuity between their past and future existences.

Even upon reaching Britain, the desire for positive affirmation persisted, and stable communication allowed the returning soldiers more opportunities to assert their presence in their families' lives. The process of rehabilitation extended beyond physical recovery to include emotional reintegration into civilian life, emphasising the importance of maintaining connections with loved ones throughout the transitional period.

Once the men had settled into their accommodations, various activities were made available to them before they departed for home. Alongside granting each man 28 days of leave and a daily allowance, the Education and Rehabilitation Service (ERS) took on the responsibility of facilitating the men's reintegration into civilian life. The ERS provided educational courses and professional development opportunities for those interested in utilising their time in Britain productively. Work placements with local firms were also arranged, offering the men voluntary programs to engage in as part of their rehabilitation in Britain.

In New Zealand, the press picked up on this theme and lauded the provision of these work placements, enthusiastically sharing stories of the men's success and eagerness to participate. An example highlighted a warrant officer, previously employed by the Automobile Association, gaining experience at Fanim House in London. The report emphasised the diverse aspects of his work, from local and foreign travel to insurance and the handling of vehicle transport and road services. The individual's renewed confidence and commitment to forgo leave upon returning to New Zealand underscored the positive impact of these programs. The press's optimistic portrayal aimed to shape public opinion, emphasising that the men were not merely holidaying but actively working towards becoming productive citizens upon their return.

While the ERS aimed to help POWs spend their time productively, Arthur Coe's experience revealed a different side. Coe, aspiring to start a medical career, was disheartened when his rehabilitation officer rejected his application. Despite Coe's background working in camp hospitals and studying medical textbooks, the officer dismissed his experience, viewing him as lacking formal education. The realisation that his efforts during imprisonment were deemed meaningless post-captivity was crushing. The liberation he had envisioned as an opportunity to pursue his dreams turned out to be restricted by post-war limitations. Unbound by physical constraints, Coe still felt confined by the disappointment, prompting him to flee his rehabilitation centre and go AWOL, taking a train to London.

Coe's journey, gazing at the serene English countryside, highlighted the contrast between external tranquillity and internal despair. Despite vocational setbacks, his regained mobility provided a sense of agency. However, the symbolism of being behind the carriage window echoed a lingering prison motif, emphasising that the peaceful world he had envisioned was tantalizingly close but still out of reach.

Coe's resistance to the limitations imposed during rehabilitation appeared to be a shared sentiment among other prisoners. The New Zealand Herald highlighted that POWs exhibited a strong determination to distance themselves as far as possible from their camp environments. The article noted a prevalent trend of prisoners obtaining railway vouchers for Inverness, one of the farthest travel points, with many actually visiting Scotland. The return from leave, marked not only by increased self-confidence but also a willingness to settle down and await transportation, reflected the POWs' desire for freedom and exploration.

For POWs, the joy of being able to move freely was paramount, irrespective of whether the journey took them near or far. Warrant Officer Charles Croall, recalling his time at Brighton, vividly described the intoxicating experience of walking where he pleased, revelling in the sight of street lights after nearly three years of blackout conditions. Croall's account conveyed a profound sense of liberation, almost like an out-of-body experience. The absence of guard towers and barbed wire removed the previous constraints, opening up a world that was once restricted. While his walk might have seemed aimless, it symbolised a significant expression of freedom.

The imagery of street lights held particular significance, offering a stark contrast to the conditions endured in prison camps. Against the backdrop of captivity and the war-torn landscape of Europe, the brilliance of these lights symbolised a return to civilisation. Croall's experience encapsulated the contrast between the darkness of confinement and the newfound freedom illuminated by the street lights, emphasising the prisoners' journey back to a semblance of normalcy.

For POWs grappling with the challenge of assimilating into their unfamiliar surroundings, the quest for distractions became a welcome refuge. Despite occasional moments of enjoyment, the aspiration to leave behind memories of their captivity was consistently disrupted by persistent reminders of their harrowing experiences. Every day, seemingly mundane occurrences had the power to trigger intense recollections, mentally transporting the men back to the confines of their prison camps. Captain Osborn Jones shared his experience:

"This morning, I took a leisurely stroll along the Embankment and other familiar parts of London. It was a splendid spring Sunday morning, and as I stood by the Thames, gazing at the magnificent Westminster building and listening to Big Ben striking the hour, I found it challenging to believe that I was truly awake. These surreal moments still loom over me, and I can't shake the lingering half-expectation... as if I might soon find myself on parade in a square somewhere in Germany."

Len ended up being billeted with a couple in London, whilst Fred was billeted out to Beryl Brown's family for the duration of their time in the UK.

Despite the considerable volume of prisoners requiring processing and transportation back to New Zealand, the majority were en route home after a mere few months of rehabilitation. Commencing in May 1945, the repatriation process progressed swiftly, and by September, only 300 individuals designated as repatriates remained in Britain.

CHAPTER 18

RETURNING HOME TO NZ

The joyous return of Len and other soldiers to New Zealand.

Reuniting with family and the challenges of readjusting to civilian life.

Kaye and Norma greeting Len at his homecoming.
© Family archives.

33517 - THE UNTOLD STORY OF PRIVATE F. L. HUTCHINSON

The shores of New Zealand greeted Len Hutchinson and his fellow soldiers with the embrace of familiarity and the echoes of joyous reunions. The return home marked the end of a tumultuous chapter in Len's life, but the challenges of readjusting to civilian life awaited, intertwined with the warmth of family and the hope for a future free from the shadows of war.

The moment Len stepped onto New Zealand soil, the air seemed charged with anticipation and the promise of homecoming. The joyous reunions with family and loved ones became the focal point of a nation eager to welcome back its heroes. For Len, the sight of familiar faces and the embrace of loved ones offered a balm for the wounds of war.

Reuniting with his beloved Norma and their daughter Kaye was a poignant moment in Len's journey. The family, now reshaped by the passage of time and the trials of war, embodied the hope for a future free from the constraints of conflict. Len's doting mother, sisters, and brothers, along with the extended family, added layers of support and love, creating a tapestry of connection that would aid in the process of healing.

Reunited with Norma and friends. © Family archives.

Len found solace and stability in the embrace of his family. He, Norma, and Kaye returned to the fold of his mother's home, a sanctuary where the wounds of war could be tended to with the tenderness of familial care. The transition from the rigid routines of military life to the comforting chaos of family life was not without its challenges, but the Hutchinsons faced them with a resilience honed in the crucible of war.

The shadows of war, however, lingered in Len's psyche. Night terrors, the silent echoes of the battlefield, and the weight of shell shock—what would later be recognised as post-traumatic stress disorder (PTSD)—became silent companions in the quiet moments of civilian life. The struggle to reconcile the past with the present, though invisible to many, added layers of complexity to Len's journey of readjustment.

Len's departure from the military marked a shift in his career path. Embracing a new chapter, he became a cook for Chelsea Sugar Works—a tangible step toward normalcy and routine. The rhythms of civilian employment, coupled with the support of his family, provided a semblance of stability for Len as he navigated the challenges of post-war life.

In roughly a year, Len and Norma expanded their family with the arrival of another baby daughter, Rayna. The laughter of children and the responsibilities of parenthood became integral components of Len's post-war narrative, contributing to the process of rebuilding a life beyond the confines of conflict.

The Hutchinsons, like many families of returning soldiers, faced the complexities of reintegration. The scars of war, both visible and hidden, were woven into the fabric of their daily lives. Yet, within the embrace of family and the shared determination to move forward, the Hutchinsons crafted a narrative of resilience, recovery, and the enduring capacity for love.

Len Hutchinson's journey from the battlefields of North Africa and the frozen landscapes of the Long March to the warmth of his family's hearth in New Zealand symbolised not just a physical return but a triumph of the human spirit over the trials of war. The Hutchinson family, like the nation they called home, embarked on a journey of rebuilding—a journey that would shape the legacy of Len and his fellow soldiers, leaving an indelible mark on the pages of New Zealand's post-war history.

CHAPTER 19

LIFE AND LEGACY

Len's journey continued beyond the confines of war, and he played a pivotal role in uniting two families when he introduced his war buddy Fred, the gentle giant, to Norma's sister, Tuppy. The unexpected outcome: Fred becoming his brother-in-law, added a unique chapter to Len's post-war life.

Returning to civilian life, alongside his Sugar Works job and his family, they moved out of their shared accommodation with Len's mother, May, and would eventually purchase a house on Palmerston Road, Birkenhead.

Len took up working at the Northcote Tavern, affectionately known as 'The Trough'. This place would become a mainstay in the family for generations to come.

The couple embraced a love for travel, making an annual pilgrimage to the far north, specifically Matauri Bay. There, they camped for at least three weeks, immersing themselves in the beauty of nature and engaging with the local community. Their affinity for exploration extended to Treasure Island, Fiji, where they made several memorable visits.

A significant chapter unfolded when Len and Norma travelled to Bougainville to spend time with their daughter Rayna and her family during a two-year stint there. The couple also ventured south to Rotorua as Rayna and her family relocated, further enriching their experiences.

Len and Norma's nomadic spirit found expression in the purchase of a pop-up camper, facilitating frequent journeys north to visit Kaye and her family on their farm. Alongside his friend Fred, Len developed a shared passion for making homebrew, an endeavour that added its own flavour to their shared memories.

Fred and Tuppy on the front deck of the family home.
© Family Archives.

33517 - THE UNTOLD STORY OF PRIVATE F. L. HUTCHINSON

Fred and his pen friend Beryl Brown remained in contact for the rest of Fred's life. The generational friendship is still intact to this day, across the many miles and years that have gone by since the war.

Len's legacy lives on through his surviving family members—daughters Kaye and Rayna; grandchildren Laurie, Tony, Sandi, Luke, Sarah, Megan, and Rachel; great-grandchildren Stephanie, Julianna, Sammy, Phoebe, Tara, Angus, McKenzie, Cooper, Ohio, Franco, and great-great-grandson Jaxson. In these cherished connections, Len's rich and diverse life continues to echo through the generations.

PRIVATE F.L. HUTCHINSON

REFERENCES

Prisoners of War by W. Wynne Mason
Fernlead Cairo by Alex Hedley
18 Battalion and Armoured Regiment by W.D. Dawson
Battle of Egypt by J.L. Scoullar
The Relief of Tobruk by W.E. Murphy
Il Campo "P.G. 57" a Premariacco by Natale Zaccuri
Family Stories Before and After the Internet by Kaye Clewett
Ministry of Information Photo Division
Canadian Battlefield Tours
Ferdinando Nadalutti
H.R. Dixon
M. Lee Hill
www.nzhistory.govt.nz
www.archives.govt.nz
National Library of New Zealand
Alex Hedley Snr
Hutchinson Family Archives
Ross Watson
Alexander Turnbull Library
Wikipedia
Halfway Home – The Rehabilitation of New Zealand Second World War POWs in Britain by Matthew Johnson
www.discovergerlitz.com/stalag/

www.aucklandmuseum.com/collections/
www.aifpow.com
www.nzetc.victoria.ac.nz
www.kiwiveterans.co.nz
https://www.bbc.co.uk/history/ww2peopleswar/stories/07/a7261607.shtml
http://www.buckdenpike.co.uk/lamsdorfmarch.html
https://www.iwm.org.uk/collections/search?query=NZ%20repatriates%20arrive%20in%20England
https://www.nzgeo.com/stories/the-fate-of-the-nino-bixio/
https://www.stuff.co.nz/dominion-post/news/local-papers/the-wellingtonian/4108345/Remembering-the-Nino-Bixio-dead

ABOUT THE AUTHOR

Sandi K. Wilson is a devoted child of God, a wife happily married to her fellow adventurer, a loving mother of grown children, and a proud Safta (grandmother). A passionate writer and blogger, her love of words has been a lifelong companion.

Sandi began with a blog, but it was her deeply personal books that carved her path: one about her father's journey with dementia, another about her grandfather's plight as a POW in WWII, and several stand-alone works exploring themes of faith, courage, and healing.

She is currently writing *The House of Adonai*—a visionary series of spiritual allegories—and continues to publish through her own imprint, *SKW Publishing*. Her stories invite readers into worlds marked by truth, beauty, and grace.

When she isn't writing, Sandi enjoys travelling, gardening, genealogy, and immersing herself in history and archaeology. She finds the greatest joy in spending time with her loved ones and weaving together faith, heritage, and adventure in both her life and work.

Connect with Sandi:
- **Website:** www.skwpublishing.com
- **Books:** www.sandikwilson.com

www.ingramcontent.com/pod-product-compliance
Lightning Source LLC
Chambersburg PA
CBHW071359080526
44587CB00017B/3132